世界文化遗产　A WORLD HERTAGE SITE

苏州园林
Gardens of Suzhou

陈健行　摄影

中国旅游出版社

美在诗情画意中

——为陈健行《苏州园林》摄影画册作

金学智

雨晴山远近，秋高树参差。

小桥独钓处，斜阳总是诗。

明代为拙政园作画题诗的吴门画家文征明的这首五绝，不但是一首题画诗，而且可看作是一首咏园诗。试想，在园林里，山石远近，碧树参差，小桥横斜，朱栏曲折，在夕阳余晖映照下，廊引人随，峰回路转，眼前不是一幅幅色彩明丽的画，一首首意趣隽永的诗么？

苏州园林里的日月光华，是诗人，是画家，它把处处景物染上了美丽动人的影调。

在拙政园东部，旭日始旦，朝晖已穿过树丛涂抹于廊墙，斟酌浓淡，剂量浅深，间以一个个大小不同的亮点，其艺术构成，令人想起伦勃朗(Rembrandt Harmensz Van Rijn)油画中的透明阴影和高光效果；

在拙政园中部，西下的夕阳将余晖映于水池，由于波光明灭，漪澜随风，水中倒影包括凉亭秋树无不屈曲、摇曳、聚合、分散、碎杂、拉长、扩展，互为镶嵌，相与融和……一幅橙黄色调的明莹画面，摇漾出"落日水溶金"的诗意之美；

在狮子林，久雨新晴的阳光将那挂落优美的图案、树枝屈曲的线条、栏杆雅致的结构，统统投影于廊庑的壁间、地面，并使它们上下相映，明暗交融，俨然一幅具象与抽象渗化交织的绝妙画卷，真是雨后复斜阳，水晕化墨章；

在艺圃，芹庐小院有大片粉墙，日光筛下的树影，疏疏的叶，弯弯的枝，这是以渲染手法绘就的一幅"天开图画"，画出了"粉墙花影自重重"的名句意境……

日光，是美的；月色，更迷人。且不说网师园的月到风来亭幻引了多少摄影家审美的目光，就说其他园林，虎丘有揽月池，耦园有受月池，怡园有锄月轩，艺圃有响月廊，一个"响"字特富诗意，故而廊内有联曰："踏月寻诗临碧沼……"

在苏州园林，光与影有着丰富的表现：台阶前，曲栏旁，小溪边，山路上，那婆娑的花树，虬结的藤廊，雅致的栏辈，精美的漏窗，滤下了月华和日光，于是，到处金斑点点，银丝缕缕，阴阳相杂，不可名状，如音阶的高低，如旋律的抑扬，如乐思的呈现，如调性的升降，如织体的流动，如八音的交响，这种光影错综的协奏曲，是无声之音，无色之相。于是，一些古诗名句也会跃进人们脑际："月移花影上栏杆"，"云破月来花弄影"，"疏影横斜水清浅"，"明月松间照，清泉石上流"……

怡园，有"四时潇洒"之亭，亭名诗意地点出了苏州园林春夏秋冬四季的潇洒风流。

春天，近水花先发。网师园池畔向水的繁枝上，密缀着以素馨迎春的绿叶黄花；而枝拂池面，又可见"风乍起，吹绉一池春水"。在拙政园、狮子林水池旁，柳枝纤弱修长，倒垂金线，猗傩多姿，柔情万千；而远观则又烟蔼蔼，雾蒙蒙，犹如细雨迷漫，薄纱轻笼。这些，都是吟诗作画的好题材：或"嫩于金色软于丝"，或"柳絮池塘淡淡风"，或"万条垂下绿丝绦"，或"惯得轻柔绮陌中"……

入夏，昼永堪寻幽。留园"小蓬莱"的曲桥藤架上，绿叶丛丛，紫英累累，鲜艳照眼明，给人以喜悦，予人以温馨，它是自然繁华之画，生命充实之诗。而拙政园的满池荷花，"出淤泥而不染，濯清涟而不妖"，绿意红情，香远益清，还令人想起"碧叶喜翻风，红英宜照日"的诗句来。

深秋，一夜西风向池塘。留园冠云峰独立寒秋，与东篱黄菊为伴，超拔群峰外，孤秀白云中。而留园、怡园、听枫园的枫叶尽染，绚林如醉，"霜叶红于二月花"；沧浪亭清香馆、怡园金粟亭、留香园闻木樨香轩，又金银缀满枝头，令人想起计成《园冶》的美言："冉冉天香，悠悠桂子……"

寒冬，木叶萧萧凝冷韵。当一场瑞雪降临后，眼前就出现岑参笔下的奇景："忽如一夜春风来，千树万树梨花开。"在拙政园香洲一带，翼然的屋顶、精致的低栏、曲折的石岸、多姿的树木，无不因飞英的委积而洁白皑皑，一派清辉。这里，琼楼玉宇，琪花瑶草，一切的一切，都静静地融进了银色的梦。

留园有"佳晴喜雨快雪"之亭，概括说明了苏州园林不仅四季皆宜，而且晴雨皆美。晴日，有清晰明艳之美；雨天，有模糊虚幻之美，所谓"水光潋滟晴方好，山色空蒙雨亦奇"。蒙蒙细雨，把沧浪亭水面更推向虚无不定的远方，于是，亭廊隐约现，背景有无中，构成一幅淋漓渗化的水墨画。淅沥疏雨，拙政园听雨轩外，则是蕉叶竹叶皆响，大珠小珠俱走，静听天地之清籁，动人诗情，兴人乐感！雨过天晴，苏州诸园的地面文章——花街铺地，经雨水冲刷，又变得毫无纤尘，晶莹透亮，图案精细匀齐，色调文静雅丽，所谓"吟花席地，醉月铺毡"，是享受这"选鹅子铺成蜀锦"的工艺之美。

晨雾溟濛，"乍若飞烟散，时如佳气新"。此刻，不论是环秀山庄的湖石假山、耦园的黄石假山，还是狮子林潭旁的"小赤壁"，怡园"抱绿湾"的水门……其近景尚可辨识，中景已趋朦胧，它们随着远景一起消溶在隐约的浅灰统调之中。试看画面的景物，虽有而疑无，虽无而似有，依稀、空蒙、蒸腾、飘浮、升华……一切都淡化了，一切也诗化了。此情此景，用计成《园冶》的话说，是"动'江流天地外'之情，合'山色有无中'之句"。而怡园池上白皮松，横空飞渡，屈曲伸展于缥缈的流云游雾中，恰如惊虬拗怒，又似神龙腾舞，蔚为罕见的奇观！

苏州园林里的花木禽鱼，也极富诗情画意。且不说梅兰竹菊，岁寒三友的比德之美，就说其单纯的景观，或杂树参天，繁花覆地；或红衣出水，碧玉轻摇；或垂丝依依，落花片片；或林茂竹修，柳暗花明；或树梢莺歌，草间虫鸣；或游鱼唼喋，鸳鸯戏水……都足以触景生奇，含情多致，可谓姹紫嫣红，错综成文，莫非是画；嫩黄新绿，相媚成趣，无不是诗；松风竹响，铮琮成韵，悉皆是乐……

苏州园林里的亭台楼阁，和谐地生长在优美的生态环境，深深地吐纳着浓郁的书卷气息，它陈设高雅，室庐清靓，亭台具旷士之怀，斋馆有幽人之致，处身其中，放眼窗外，画框中人与自然可亲切地对话，情往似赠，兴来如答，臻于诗画交融、天人合一之境。

法国大雕塑家罗丹(Auguste Rodin)说："对于我们的眼睛，不是缺少美，而是缺少发现。"是的，在苏州园林里，对于如织的游人、特别是匆匆的过客来说，不是缺少诗情画意之美，而是缺少一颗诗心去体味，缺少一双画眼去观照，一句话，是缺少发现。

著名园林摄影家陈健行先生，沉浸于园林中，涵泳乎诗画间，朝于斯，夕于斯，积三十年之经验，其诗心画眼，通过摄影镜头捕捉到了苏州园林无数诗情画意之美，精选结集成这本《苏州园林》画册。这本画册以味之不尽的意境、幽雅迷人的风韵显示了一条颠扑不破的艺术原理：美在诗情画意中。

BEAUTY IN POETIC IMAGERY

— Preface to Chen Jianxing's Photo Album

Gardens of Suzhou

By Jin Xuezhi

*Mountains either far or near emerge when it
   becomes clear after rain;*
Trees vary in height in the meek autumn.
*Angling alone by the small bridge and seeing the
   waning sun,*
*You can't help feeling overwelmed by the poetic
   aura.*

The poem by Wen Zhenming, an artist of the Wu School of Painting who contributed poems and paintings to the creation of the Humble Administrator's Garden in the Ming Dynasty, not only describes a painting, but also depicts the garden. When we contemplate the scenes in the classical gardens, the groves and rocks far and near, green foliages at varying height, delicate zigzag bridges spanning the waters, red balustrades and corridors under the setting sun meandering through mountain ridges, aren't we discovering a series of brightly tinted pictures, as well as poems of intriguing imagery?

Like the poet and painter, the light of daytime and night casts a moving tone of hues over the scenes of the classical gardens.

In the eastern section of the Humble Administrator's Garden, the morning sun infiltrates the groves and projects the shadows on the walls and verandahs in different shades, leaving big and small bright spots, which call to mind the highly contrasting effect of translucent shades and strong light in the oil paintings of Rembrandt Harmensz Van Rijn.

In the central section of the Humble Administrator's Garden, the setting sun sheds its fading light across the glistening ripples of the pond in breeze, where the reflections of pavilions and autumn trees bend and sway, gather and disperse, then fall scattered, stretched, and intermingled, culminating in a painting of golden orange tone that reveals the poetic beauty of "gold melted in the waters under the setting sun".

In the Lion Grove Garden, when the fresh sunshine after a long span of rain casts the shadows of the elegantly carved door frames, the curved branches, and the elegant woodwork of balustrade upon the walls and floor, there is an interacting between those above and those below, and between light and shade in a wonderful scroll which combines the concrete with the abstract, wherein the rain stains evaporate into an ink and wash.

In the Garden of Herbs, a massive wall in the Court of Qinlu, presents a natural painting of tree shadows, dispersed leaves, curved branches sifted through the sunshine, just like an ink and wash by "the hand of nature", as a famous line goes, "Layers after layers of flowers are brushed onto the white washed walls."

The light of daytime is attractive, but the glow of the moon can be more enchanting. Apart from the Pavilion of Breeze in Moon-lit Night in the Master-of-Nets Garden, there are spots in other gardens associated with the moon, such as the Moon Fetching Pond on the Tiger Hill, the Moon-lit Pond in the Garden of Couple's Retreat, and the Corridor of Resounding Moon in the Garden of Herbs. The word "resounding" is used in a poetic sense, as revealed in the couplet inside the corridor, "I search the poetic inspiration under the moon and find myself facing the pool of green waters."

Light and shadows are richly reflected in Suzhou classical gardens: in front of stone steps, by the winding balustrade, along the creeks, or by the mountain paths, the light of the sun or the moon comes through the blooming trees, the arcade of creeping plants, the elegantly shaped wooden balustrade, and the exquisite latticed windows, etc. Everywhere are spots of gold and silver interwoven in light and shade, just like musical notes in the rise and fall , the change of rhythm and the variation of tones, and the mixing of sounds. All this seems to form a concerto of light and shade . Immediately reminiscent are such lines from classical poems as: "The shadows of flowers climb up the balustrade as the moon is afloat," "As the moon peeps through the clouds, the flowers play with their shadows," "Shadows sway in the limped shallow waters," and "The bright moon infiltrates the pines to cast light on the jasper spring spilling over rocks."

In the Garden of Harmony there is a pavilion named "Grace of Four Seasons", which points to the fact that scenes in Suzhou classical gardens excel in all seasons of the year.

In spring, flowers near waters come out first. Fragrant yellow flowers bloom on the cascading twigs of green leaves sweeping over the pond of the Master-of-Nets Garden. The twigs caress the waters as "the light breeze raises slow ripples in the pond." In the Humble Administrator's Garden and the Lion Grove Garden, the weeping willows with sprouting leaves on drooping twigs swing over the waters, looking like drizzling in a haze or a colossal light gauze. All this is the favorite topic for poets and painters: "Tender as the melting gold and soft as silk," "The light willows over the breezy waters," "Thousands of silk-like strands drooping over the pond," or "Soft and mellow in the delicate land."

In summer, silence descends in the deep night. Green leaves and purple flowers multiply on the wisteria trellis over the zigzag bridge of the "Petty Penglai" in the Lingering Garden. The magnificent and pleasant sight, like the robust work of art by nature and poem of lively spirit, fills the mind with joy and warmth. The lotus flowers that crowd the pond of the Humble Administrator's Garden in red against green, "coming out of mud but spotlessly clean, and elegant but not flirtatious," send their fragrance far and wide. The line comes to the mind that "Green leaves enjoy the company of breeze, while red flowers stand out in sunlight."

In deep autumn, west wind blows over the pond. The Cloud-Crowned Peak in the Lingering Garden stands erect in lonely height under white clouds and accompanied by yellow chrysanthemums. The frost-etched maples in the Lingering Garden, the Garden of harmony, and the Garden of Whispering Maples turn flaming red, which "outshine the early spring flowers". By the Hall of Refreshing Fragrance in the Surging Waves Pavilion, the Golden Grain Pavilion of the Garden of Harmony, and the Osmanthus Pavilion of the Lingering Garden, the golden and silvery osmanthus blooms in abundance, reminding people of Ji Cheng's description in his "On Gardening", "Sweet scent fills the air, and delicate osmanthus flowers beckon admirers."

The freezing winter strips trees of leaves in cold air. After a snowfall appears what Cen Can calls the spectacular scene: "As if by a blast of spring wind overnight, all the trees are strewn with pear blossoms." Around the "Fragrant Isle" in the Humble Administrator's Garden, the roofs, the delicate stone balustrade, the rocky edges of the pond, the trees of multifarious shapes are all covered with glistening white snow, and the buildings and plants immersed in a silvery dreamland.

In the Lingering Garden, there is a pavilion called "Pleasure in Sun, Rain, and Snow", which sums up the charm of Suzhou classical gardens in all seasons and weathers: clear and bright in sunshine, and hazy and blurry in rain, as the line goes, "pretty reflections of colours in water under the sun, and rare scene of the mountains enveloped in a rainy mist." The stream of the Surging Waves Pavilion seems to drift into the unknown, and the silhouette of corridor and pavilions against a dim background creates a painting of ink and wash. Outside the Hall of Splattering Rain in the Humble Administrator's Garden, a symphony of sounds of the rain drops blown on bamboo and banana leaves purifies the mind for nature's music and poetry. Then, the rain-washed mosaic paving of pebble stones in the gardens, bright and free from dust, can compare to the exquisitely designed brocade or carpet. Behold the scenes of the rockery in the Garden of Secluded Beauty, the yellow granite artificial hill in the Garden of Couple's Retreat, the "Petty Chibi" by the pond of the Lion Grove Garden, and the water grotto at the "Green Girdled Bay" in the Garden of Harmony! Clearly visible at close-up, they fade out in the distance in a light grayish tone of poetic setting, to fit into what Ji Cheng describes in his "On Gardening" as the "waters from nowhere" and "mountains in transient existence". In the Garden of Harmony, the white-barked pines spread the sturdy boughs cross the pond to make a unique scene of dragons soaring in clouds.

The flavour of poetry and painting can also be felt in the plants, birds, and fishes in suzhou classical gardens. Apart from the plum blossoms, orchids, bamboos, and chrysanthemums, and the "three companions of winter", there are scenes like towering trees and exuberant flower-beds, red lilies on water surface and swaying white lotus, dangling twigs and fallen flower petals, tree and bamboo groves that deepen the perspective, the twittering birds and insects, the swimming fishes and frolicking mandarin ducks, etc., which trigger off one's imaginations and impulse for poetry and painting with the blending of colours and sounds.

The architectural forms in Suzhou classical gardens, the pavilions, terraces, and towers, are harmoniously fitted into the beautiful ecological environs of scholarly taste. The elegantly furnished halls and lounges offer quiet retreat while pavilions and terraces command superb views. Looking through the windows, one seems to communicate with nature in an intimate manner. Here, the poetry and painting, man and nature are melted into one harmonious whole.

The great French sculptor Auguste Rodin once said, "What is lacking in our eyes is not beauty, but discovery." Indeed, to the swarms of visitors to Suzhou classical gardens, especially to those hurrying through, the garden is never short of poetic and picturesque beauty, but the poetic mind to savour it, and the artist's eye to appreciate it, in a word, the power to discover.

Mr. Chen Jianxing, a well-known photographer, has for over thirty years been devoted to the art of Suzhou classical gardens from a poetic approach and, with his artist outlook and poetic mind, captured numerous scenes with his camera, whence have come the photos for the current album, "Gardens in Poetic Sentiments", through the most scrutinizing selection. It is by the compelling artistic charm of the album that beauty is conceived in the poetic imagery.

春来发几枝（网师园） The Master-of-Nets Garden

无数蝉鸣翠扫空（拙政园） The Humble Administrator's Garden

萧萧黄叶落无声（狮子林）　The Lion Grove Garden

奇石含尽千古秀 （狮子林） The Lion Grove Garden

几处早莺争暖树（拙政园）　The Humble Administrator's Garden

薄雾笼远树（拙政园）　The Humble Administrator's Garden

珠帘凝翠露华浓 （狮子林） The Lion Grove Garden

嫣红映晚霞 （拙政园）　The Humble Administrator's Garden

春色满园尽朝晖（拙政园） The Humble Administrator's Garden

绿扬宜作两家春 （拙政园）　The Humble Administrator's Garden

谁家新燕衔春泥 （拙政园） The Humble Administrator's Garden

艳如霞光殷于火 （拙政园）　The Humble Administrator's Garden

贴水楼台先得月 （退思园）　The Garden of Meditation

嫩于金色软于丝（拙政园） The Humble Administrator's Garden

春暖早添绿（留　园）　The Lingering Garden

清风穿庭时带香（拙政园）　The Humble Administrator's Garden

逗得春水上枝条（退思园）　The Garden of Meditation

曲桥贴碧水（艺 圃） The Garden of Herbs

小庭长对四时花（怡　园）　The Garden of Harmony

花气三月浮香霭（沧浪亭） The Surging Waves Pavilion

鸟鸣山愈静（拙政园） The Humble Administrator's Garden

露唏向晚 （拙政园）　The Humble Administrator's Garden

日高花影重（网师园） The Master-of-Nets Garden

春园游人宜带雨 （沧浪亭） The Surging Waves Pavilion

园色深浅随夕照（拙政园）　The Humble Administrator's Garden

斜日到窗前（拙政园） The Humble Administrator's Garden

且教桃李闹春风（留　园）　The Lingering Garden

春晓鸟鸣晴（留　园）　The Lingering Garden

花影习习春（拙政园） The Humble Administrator's Garden

春日融融海棠红（拙政园） The Humble Administrator's Garden

小庭贮幽香（留　园）　The Lingering Garden

满架紫英—院香（留 园） The Lingering Garden

柳絮池塘淡淡风 （拙政园）The Humble Administrator's Garden

夜来风雨声（拙政园）　The Humble Administrator's Garden

四壁荷花三面柳 （拙政园）　The Humble Administrator's Garden

水清鱼争跃（留　园）　The Lingering Garden

绿肥红瘦春已深（拙政园）　The Humble Administrator's Garden

曙光透绮窗（狮子林） The Lion Grove Garden

上有黄鹂深树鸣（狮子林） The Lion Grove Garden

山幽鸟谈天（拙政园）　The Humble Administrator's Garden

田田舒新荷（拙政园）　The Humble Administrator's Garden

映带晚霞—抹红（留　园）　The Lingering Garden

月到风来水生凉（拙政园）　The Humble Administrator's Garden

一湾清泉总宜诗（环秀山庄） The Garden of Secluded Beauty

花影扶疏上西窗 （耦 园） The Garden of Couple's Retreat

鸟语报春晴（拙政园）　The Humble Administrator's Garden

小院深明别有天（拙政园）　The Humble Administrator's Garden

帘虚日薄花竹影（耦　园）　The Garden of Couple's Retreat

一片冰心在玉壶（拙政园）　The Humble Administrator's Garden

室虚待婵娟（耦　园）　The Garden of Couple's Retreat

玉宇净无尘（耦园） The Garden of Couple's Retreat

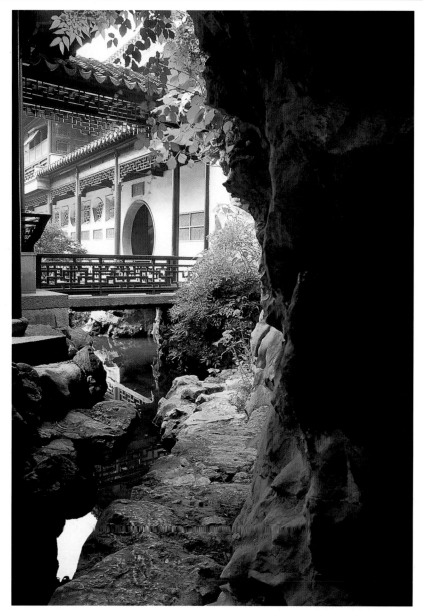

几处娇莺语正酣　（环秀山庄）The Garden of Secluded Beauty

绿荫小憩始觉凉（留　园）　The Lingering Garden

雨过富声远 （拙政园）The Humble Administrator's Garden

步步踏断蛙鼓　（艺　圃）The Garden of Herbs

一湾小溪出幽林（拙政园）　The Humble Administrator's Garden

满洒金色上檐头（怡 园） The Garden of Harmony

晓来谁染霜林醉 （拙政园）The Humble Administrator's Garden

江南亭榭梦魂萦 （留　园）　The Lingering Garden

锦鳞潜池嬉秋亭（拙政园） The Humble Administrator's Garden

枝叶疏疏落粉墙（艺　圃）　The Garden of Herbs

叶叶落去可数红（听枫园） The Garden of Whispering Maples

连日秋雨黄叶飞（狮子林） The Lion Grove Garden

风露入新秋（狮子林） The Lion Grove Garden

园幽斜晖暖（拙政园） The Humble Administrator's Garden

寂寂轩窗淡淡影 （拙政园）The Humble Administrator's Garden

日月长相留（怡 园） The Garden of Harmony

相对无言（沧浪亭） The Surging Waves Pavilion

回廊挹爽映斜阳（沧浪亭） The Surging Waves Pavilion

秋霜染得万树金（狮子林） The Lion Grove Garden

晨起步回廊（拙政园）　The Humble Administrator's Garden

一抹夕阳窗影斜（耦　园）　The Garden of Couple's Retreat

斜日霭深（留 园） The Lingering Garden

霜重叶更红（拙政园） The Humble Administrator's Garden

絮语西窗下（沧浪亭）　The Surging Waves Pavilion

梧桐叶疏秋已深（怡　园）　The Garden of Harmony

霜叶红于二月花（怡　园）　The Garden of Harmony

秋落香洲胜春光（拙政园） The Humble Administrator's Garden

沧浪展印有无中（沧浪亭）　The Surging Waves Pavilion

秋荷秋水夕照红（拙政园） The Humble Administrator's Garden

庭雪先开玉树花（网师园）　The Master-of-Nets Garden

闲敲棋子落灯花（拙政园）　The Humble Administrator's Garden

千朵万朵压枝低（狮子林）　The Lion Grove Garden

晴雪晓寒薄（拙政园） The Humble Administrator's Garden

一夜西风向池塘（留　园）　The Lingering Garden

寒梅已作东风信（网师园） The Master-of-Nets Garden

坐听松风起涛声（怡　园）　The Garden of Harmony

依依小亭映新晴（拙政园）　The Humble Administrator's Garden

晓雾迷蒙人语稠（狮子林） The Lion Grove Garden

一泓池水映雪晴（网师园）　The Master-of-Nets Garden

顾　　问: 丁宝联
责任编辑: 龚威健
摄　　影: 陈健行
撰　　文: 金学智
英　　文: 沈仲辉
英文译审: 程伟进
装帧设计: 陈晓冰
版式制作: 于　伟

图书在版编目(CIP)数据

苏州园林: 中、英文对照/陈健行摄影.
－北京: 中国旅游出版社 2000.5
ISBN 7-5032-1730-8

Ⅰ.苏 … Ⅱ.陈… Ⅲ. 古典园林－江苏
－苏州市－摄影集 Ⅳ.K928.73-64

中国版本图书馆CIP数据核字 (2000) 第 08100 号

《苏州园林》
出版发行: 中国旅游出版社
地　　址: 北京建国门内大街甲九号
邮　　编: 100005
制　　版: 深圳利丰雅高电分制版有限公司
印　　刷: 东莞新扬印刷有限公司
版　　次: 2000 年 5 月第 1 版
印　　次: 2000 年 5 月第 1 版　第 1 次
开　　本: 850 × 1168 毫米　　1/24
印　　张: 4　　　　　　005800